JB JOSSEY-BASS

THE MOST EXTREME BUGS

Animal Planet

By Catherine Nichols

Foreword by Kevin Mohs and Ian McGee

BICENTENNIAL
1807
WILEY
2007
BICENTENNIAL

John Wiley & Sons, Inc.

Published by Jossey-Bass
A Wiley Imprint
989 Market Street, San Francisco, CA 94103-1741
www.josseybass.com

Developed by Nancy Hall, Inc.
Photo research by Linda Falken
Designed by Alisa Komsky and Tom Koken
Cover design by Alisa Komsky

DCI Book Development Team
Maureen Smith, Executive Vice President & General Manager, Animal Planet
Kevin Mohs, Vice President, Animal Genre, Discovery US Networks Production
Peggy Ang, Vice President, Animal Planet Marketing
Ian McGee, Series Producer, Natural History New Zealand
Carol LeBlanc, Vice President, Licensing
Elizabeth Bakacs, Vice President, Creative Services
Caitlin Erb, Licensing Specialist

Jossey-Bass books and products are available through most bookstores. To contact Jossey-Bass directly, call our Customer Care Department within the U.S. at 800-956-7739, outside the U.S. at 317-572-3986, or fax 317-572-4002.

Jossey-Bass also publishes its books in a variety of electronic formats. Some content that appears in print may not be available in electronic books.

Library of Congress Cataloging-in-Publication Data

Nichols, Catherine.
  Animal planet : the most extreme bugs / by Catherine Nichols ; foreword by Kevin Mohs and Ian McGee. — 1st ed.
     p. cm.
  Includes index.
  ISBN: 978-0-7879-8663-6 (cloth)
  1. Insects—Juvenile literature. I. Title. II. Title: Most extreme bugs.
  QL467.2.N53 2007
  595.7—dc22
                         2006101887

Printed in China
First edition

10 9 8 7 6 5 4 3 2 1

REACH OUT. ACT. RESPOND.
Go to AnimalPlanet.com/ROAR and find out how you can be a voice for animals everywhere!

TABLE of CONTENTS

Foreword

To me, countdown shows are addictive, because I feel compelled to watch until the very end to discover who or what ranks number one in a given category—even if it's dance moves that changed the world. Given that and my knowledge of animals, it's not surprising that I decided to propose a countdown series about the most amazing behaviors and abilities of all kinds of creatures to Animal Planet. The network liked the idea, so I teamed up with Ian McGee, an entomologist turned television producer for Natural History New Zealand, who once measured caterpillar heads for a living—and *The Most Extreme* was born.

To make the series fun and interactive as well as informative, Ian and I made sure that each show had a unique ranking system that allowed us to include some of the world's most amazing animal behavior. That's how termites landed in the #1 spot in our "Builders" episode (African Macrotermes termites build mounds up to 25 feet high). *Animal Planet The Most Extreme* books follow the same format as the show and are filled with offbeat facts about animals and the astonishing things they do—such as tailor ants, which glue the leaves of their nest together by squeezing strands of silk from their own larvae; and petroleum fly larvae, which live in oil seeps and eat the bacteria that feed on the oil.

Ian, the production team, and I all share a passion for animals, so *The Most Extreme* series has been a filmmaker's dream come true, and we are delighted that there are now books based on the series. If, after watching the show or reading the books, you find yourself sharing unusual animal facts or debating the selections in a *Most Extreme* countdown with friends or family, then Ian and I feel that we have succeeded, because we've not only entertained you, but also engaged you in the extraordinary natural world that surrounds you. So get ready to take reading to the *Most Extreme* as you delve into the pages of *Animal Planet The Most Extreme Bugs*, a totally awesome book.

Sincerely,

Kevin Mohs

Executive Producer for Animal Planet

Ian McGee

Series Producer for
Natural History New Zealand

Bugs Make Headlines!

SPECIAL REPORT:
Monster 4-inch-long cockroach discovered in the wilds of Borneo!

You'd have to travel thousands of miles to see the extreme bugs in these headlines, but you can find some pretty amazing bugs in your own backyard—or home. Take the cockroach. Thousands of dollars are spent each year trying to rid homes of this extreme survivor, which can lose its head and still live for up to a week.

Just becoming a bug is extreme. Most insects grow in stages, a process called metamorphosis. Some go through three stages: eggs, nymphs (immature), and adults. Nymphs look like miniature wingless versions of their parents. They molt (shed their skin) several times before reaching adulthood. Arachnids grow this way, too, but spider babies are called spider-lings and scorpion babies are called scorplings and, of course, they never grow wings.

SPECIAL REPORT:
Trap-jaw ant from Latin America sets speed record for world's fastest bite!

Most types of insects make the journey to adulthood in four stages: eggs, larvae, pupae, and adults. Larvae look nothing like their parents. For example, caterpillars become moths or butterflies. After molting several times, a larva makes a cocoon or case for itself. Inside, the larva, now called a pupa, develops into its adult shape. When it's finished changing, the adult emerges.

Now it's time to learn some incredible facts about familiar animals as well as discover some really extreme creatures from the far corners of the Earth.

SPECIAL REPORT:
Hawaiian snail-eating caterpillar traps its victims and eats them alive!

1 STRANGE-LOOKING BUGS

All bugs may look strange to human eyes, but some bugs definitely look stranger than others. And what a group of odd-looking creatures are gathered on the next few pages! Whether they have extreme versions of familiar body parts or their own unique appendages, all ten look like they came straight out of the pages of a twisted sci-fi magazine!

#10 Hickory Horned Devil

Like many caterpillars, this larva of the regal moth sheds its skin several times as it grows. The hickory horned devil changes color each of the five times it molts, and the spiny projections along its body change shape and size as well as color. By the time the caterpillar is fully grown and ready to burrow into the ground on its way to becoming a moth, it's about 5 inches long. Though colorful and fierce-looking, this caterpillar is harmless.

#9 Hummingbird Hawk Moth

Like the hummingbird, this hawk moth is a fast flyer with a rapid wingbeat and hovers in front of a flower to dine. However, the hawk moth doesn't have a beak. Instead, it unfurls its extra-long proboscis to sip nectar. This "tongue" can measure up to 13 inches in length. When not feeding, the hawk moth rolls the tongue up to get it out of the way.

Giraffe-necked Weevil

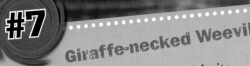

This is one beetle that really sticks its neck out—far out! The aptly named giraffe-necked weevil, a plant-eater from Madagascar, is the longest of all the weevils. The male grows to 3 inches in length and most of that length is neck. He uses his long neck to roll up leaves for his mate, who then deposits a single egg in each leaf tube.

#8

Stalk-eyed Fly

With eyes at the tips of long, slender stalks, these male flies look like something out of a horror movie. The females of the species, however, find them "beautiful," for the longer the stalks, the better the genes. Males with extra-long stalks have been found to produce more male offspring, and since female stalk-eyed flies outnumber males two to one, these eye-popping males are much in demand.

I need a REALLY long scarf.

#6

Stag Beetle

With hooked mandibles (the insect equivalent of jaws) making up almost one-third of its body length, the male stag beetle is a fierce warrior—with other male stag beetles, that is. The creature's jaws are too weak to cause humans any real pain, although the females, with smaller yet stronger jaws, have a bite that can be painful. Males defend their territory by battling other males. Each beetle tries to lock the other in his jaws and throw his competitor to the ground. The winner gets to keep his turf.

Long ago in Europe, people used stag beetles as kites, flying them on a piece of string.

THAT'S WILD!

#5

Assassin Spider

This fearsome arachnid certainly lives up to its name. It goes after its own kind, stabbing prey with the large fangs at the end of its extra-long jaws. The assassin spider has also evolved a very long neck, making it look something like a tiny crane (the kind used for building) and allowing it to strike from a distance. Of course, size and distance are relative, since the entire spider is only .8 of an inch long! This new species of assassin spider was recently discovered in Madagascar, though a few other types are found in Australia and South Africa.

Last name, Did. First name, Katy.

#4

Spiny Devil Katydid

This Central and South American rain forest dweller is covered with prickly spines sharp enough to draw blood. Only 2.5 to 3 inches long, the spiny devil katydid has even been known to use its front legs to fight off predators as large as small monkeys! During the night, males sing a high-pitched song to attract females, who put out their front legs to listen. Why? Because that's where their ears are located. Should a bat looking for a meal happen to hone in on a spiny devil katydid's song, it's in for a nasty surprise!

#3 Flatid Leaf Bug

Madagascar is home to many weird creatures, and flatid leaf bugs are no exception. Their distinction is that they look unusual both as young insects and adults. As nymphs, these spooky creatures might have just crawled out of a UFO. To deter predators, the nymphs form long strands of a waxlike substance that covers their bodies and turns them into ghostly spider-like creatures. Adult flatid leaf bugs look completely different, ugly ducklings turned into swans. With their broad, brightly colored wings, these bugs are excellent flyers.

It's really pretty when we dance.

Treehoppers

These insects are known for the wild shapes taken by the pronotum (a part of the thorax just in back of an insect's head) in some species. Tropical treehoppers in Central and South America are particularly strange-looking. The pronotum of one species looks something like a bizarre TV antenna with bulging tips and a long tail, while another looks like a somewhat misshapen horseshoe. Some of the less elaborately decorated treehoppers take the shape of bird droppings or the buds of the trees on which they live.

Like aphids, some species of treehoppers exude honeydew, a sweet substance produced from excess sap. Ants particularly like honeydew and to get it, will care for and protect the treehoppers that provide it. The ants will even use their antennae to stroke the treehoppers to encourage its production.

Give me a "C!"

Tropical planthoppers are among the most bizarre-looking creatures on Earth. These bugs are sometimes called lantern bugs from an unfounded belief that their heads glow in the dark. Lantern bugs from Indonesia and Asia usually have brightly patterned wings and long heads with short antennae beneath their eyes.

Of all the strange-looking planthoppers, the peanut-head bug takes the prize. Also called the alligator bug for its resemblance to the reptile, the peanut-head bug grows up to 4 inches long. Well camouflaged in color to blend in with the bark of trees in its home in Central and South American rain forests, this bug has plenty of other defenses. When it opens its wings, two big eyespots appear to scare away predators. And when camouflage and eyespots don't work, the peanut-head bug releases a stinky skunk-like spray to discourage predators.

The peanut-head bug's hollow head contains a sac, which the insect uses to store sucked-up tree sap.

THAT'S WILD!

SPECIAL REPORT:
Underground Monster

In 1976, a bizarre relative of crickets and grasshoppers was discovered in Queensland, Australia. Male Cooloola monsters sometimes come out at night, usually after heavy rain. About 1 inch long, they have stout bodies, short wings, and legs designed for shoveling the sandy soil in which they burrow. With their small feet, females can barely walk and spend their lives underground. •

CHAPTER 2 TINY GIANTS

Step aside and make room for the most extreme biggies of the bug world. Compared to most other animals, these creatures might be on the small side, but within their circle they carry a lot of weight. From the 3.5-inch-long wetapunga to our #1 champ, which measures a whopping 22 inches in length, these bugs are truly tiny giants.

#10

Wetapunga

This giant weta grows up to 3.5 inches long and, when pregnant, can weigh as much as 2.5 ounces—twice the weight of a mouse and to date, the heaviest recorded weight of any insect. These wingless insects, basically unchanged for millions of years, have suffered from the destruction of their habitat and the introduction of a fierce predator, the rat. Today, the wetapunga can be found only on Little Barrier Island in northern New Zealand.

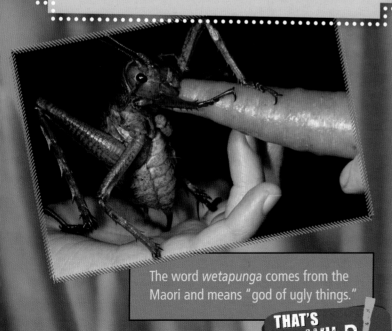

The word *wetapunga* comes from the Maori and means "god of ugly things."

THAT'S WILD!

#9

Giant Cockroach

Until recently, the giant burrowing cockroach held the record for world's largest roach. A popular pet in Australia, this wingless roach grows up to 3.5 inches long and weighs more than 1.5 ounces. Then in 2004, scientists exploring Borneo discovered a new species of cockroach. At 4 inches long, the newcomer has taken over as world's longest roach, but the giant burrowing cockroach is still world's heaviest roach.

#8

Big Beetles

Many consider the Goliath beetle of central and West Africa the world's largest beetle—and insect—in terms of body mass, which takes into account measurements of length, width, and thickness as well as density. There are, however, three other contenders for the title: a species of rhinoceros beetle found in Mexico and Central America, a rhinoceros beetle species and the titan beetle of equatorial South America.

Just call me Goliath.

#7

Long-horned Beetles

The rare titan beetle may be only one of the four largest beetles in terms of body mass, but at almost 7 inches, it definitely takes the prize for longest body. However, if you add in the length of the antennae, the prize for longest beetle might just go to the *Callipogan armillatus* beetle, whose antennae are even longer than its 5.1 inch-long body. Both beetles hail from South America.

#6

Emperor Scorpion

Although this fierce-looking scorpion is the largest of its kind, it's really quite docile. A popular pet, the emperor scorpion can grow up to 8 inches in length. Its sting, while painful, is no more harmful than a bee's. As with all scorpions, the general rule is the smaller the pincers, the more deadly the sting. A scorpion with large pincers (like the emperor scorpion) can easily kill its prey with a strong pinch, so it doesn't need a high level of toxin.

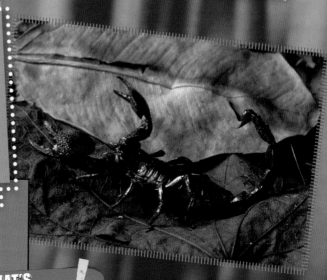

The title for world's longest scorpion belongs to the South African rock scorpion, which can reach a length of more than 8.25 inches.

THAT'S WILD!

#5 Giant Centipede

This monster of a centipede can grow up to a foot long. Found in the warm, humid forests of northwest South America, the giant centipede is an aggressive, fast-moving night hunter, attacking large spiders, lizards, rodents, and bats. Over the years, its front legs have evolved into hollow claws that are used to grasp prey and inject a large amount of strong venom. The venom can cause severe pain and flu-like symptoms in humans, though a bite is rarely fatal.

Give me an "S!"

#4 Atlas Moth

At almost 12 inches, the white witch moth of Central and South America has the longest documented wingspan of any moth. However, the prize for world's largest moth goes to the female Atlas moth of Southeast Asia, southern China, and Indonesia because, at up to 65 square inches, its wings have the largest surface area. This giant insect is no slouch as a caterpillar, either, reaching about 4.5 inches in length.

- In Taiwan, the cocoons of Atlas moths have been used as small purses.
- If a female Atlas moth lays unfertilized eggs, they will develop into males.

THAT'S WILD!

Queen Alexandra's Birdwing Butterfly

The largest butterfly in the world is the size of a small bird. Females have wingspans of up to 12 inches, while males are slightly smaller and more brightly colored. These rare butterflies are found only in the rain forests of northern Papua New Guinea and are in danger of being wiped out as the forest is cleared for farming and commercial plantations. Collectors are also to blame. Since these beautiful, exotic butterflies are so rare, specimens cost a pretty penny. Some hunters tried shooting them down with guns, but nowadays many collectors employ native New Guineans to use blowguns to capture them. Worse, the butterfly's larvae will eat only the leaves of one type of pipevine plant, severely limiting their food supply. The larvae incorporate the plant's toxins into their system, which will protect them from predators should they reach adulthood.

Discovered in 1906, this birdwing butterfly was named in honor of Queen Alexandra, wife of the United Kingdom's King Edward VII.

THAT'S WILD!

My crown keeps falling off.

Goliath Birdeater Tarantula

Despite their size, Goliath birdeater tarantulas are not aggressive to humans and are often kept as pets. If this hairy tarantula does get ticked off, it flicks bristles called urticating hairs from its abdomen at its attacker. The barbed hairs stick in skin and inside nasal passages and can be irritating as well as painful. The hairs may even cause swelling that can suffocate a small creature such as a mouse.

After stinging and paralyzing a tarantula with toxic venom, the tarantula hawk wasp drags it to its burrow, deposits an egg inside the spider's body, and seals the opening. Upon hatching, the larva devours the spider—while the spider is still alive!

THAT'S WILD!

#1 Giant Walking Stick

Found in the rain forests of Indonesia, the giant walking stick is the longest insect in the world. Most grow up to 13 inches long, although one specimen caught in Malaysia was almost 2 feet long. As its name implies, the giant walking stick resembles a stick or twig, making it almost impossible to see when it's holding as still as a statue on a woody plant. This ability to disappear into its surroundings allows the plant-eating giant walking stick to escape notice from predators, despite its size. The scientific name for this group of insects is phasmid, from the Latin for "phantom." And that's just what stick insects are—the phantoms of the bug world!

The giant walking stick also lays the largest eggs in the insect world. One egg measures .05 inches in length.

THAT'S WILD!

SPECIAL FEATURE:
World's Smallest Bug?

Okay, now you know the world's largest insect, but which one is the smallest? That honor goes to the petite fairy fly. At .0067 of an inch in length, this tiny fly is not really a fly at all. Fairy flies are a species of parasitic wasp. They lay eggs inside other insects' eggs. With such small wings, it's no surprise that fairy flies are weak fliers that are easily carried along by air currents.

CHAPTER 3 BUG BUILDERS

Be it ever so humble, there's no place like home. Some bugs, though, aren't content with simple dwellings in which to live or raise their young. They use nature's bounty to create intricate nests and webs. Others, like our #1 insect, prefer ostentatious McMansions that dominate the landscape. Prepare to meet ten of the most extreme builders of the bug world!

#9

Trapdoor Spider

Not all spiders build webs. The trapdoor spider prefers an underground abode. Besides keeping the spider safe and snug, it's an ingenious way to ambush prey. This spider digs a tunnel up to 12 inches deep and lines it with silk. The trapdoor, which gives the spider its name, is composed of silk and soil with a silk hinge. The spider waits below the trapdoor and when it feels vibrations from passing insects, it springs open the door, grabs its victim, and whisks it below to feast on.

#10

Caddisfly Larva

This underwater architect makes itself a case out of grains of sand and bits of shells, pebbles, leaves, and twigs, binding the materials together with silk that it produces from its mouth. Okay, its shelter might not win a *House Beautiful* award, but it's still home sweet home. The caddisfly larva lives in freshwater streams and ponds, where it takes its mobile home on the road, creeping along the bottom in search of food with only its head visible.

Some people make jewelry by dropping gems into a tank filled with caddisfly larvae, which then bind the gems into fashionable earrings and brooches.

THAT'S WILD!

#8

Potter Wasp

Aptly named, the female potter wasp mixes droplets of water with clay and dirt to build miniature jug-shaped nests on twigs or vines. After stocking each tiny nest with small caterpillars that she has partly paralyzed with her sting, the mother-to-be excretes a substance that she works into an upside-down cone suspended from the top of the nest. She then deposits a single egg inside and seals the nest with more mud. After the egg hatches, the wasp larva gets to feast on the still-living caterpillars as it develops into an adult.

1.

2.

3.

4.

#7

Hammock Spider

The web of this spider, although shaped like a hammock, is definitely not for dozing. It's built to help the spider catch its supper. A hammock spider runs scaffolding lines on silk above its sheet-like web. Insects become trapped in the scaffolding and fall into the hammock where the spider waits.

Watch out, Charlotte!

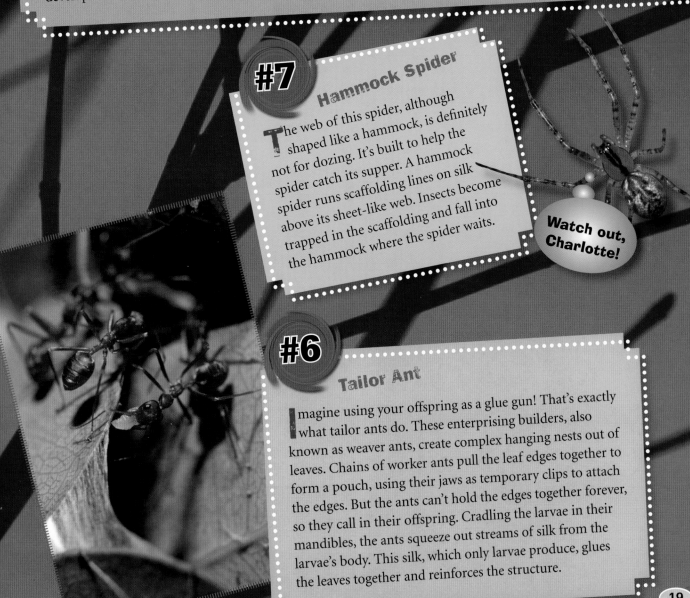

#6

Tailor Ant

Imagine using your offspring as a glue gun! That's exactly what tailor ants do. These enterprising builders, also known as weaver ants, create complex hanging nests out of leaves. Chains of worker ants pull the leaf edges together to form a pouch, using their jaws as temporary clips to attach the edges. But the ants can't hold the edges together forever, so they call in their offspring. Cradling the larvae in their mandibles, the ants squeeze out streams of silk from the larvae's body. This silk, which only larvae produce, glues the leaves together and reinforces the structure.

#5

Social Wasps

After gathering dry wood or plant fiber, social wasps (which include hornets, yellow jackets, and paper wasps) chew the material into pulp, which will harden into "paper." A queen always begins a new nest, choosing the site and building a paper stalk from which the nest will hang. She then adds six-sided cells to the stalk, lays an egg in each one, and covers the completed nest with layers of wasp paper. Once the nest is established, her young will take over the task of adding new additions and making repairs.

In New Zealand and Australia, some wasp nests are as large as a small car!

THAT'S WILD!

What a fab new yellow jacket!

#4

Honeybee

Expert engineers, honeybees manufacture honey in factory-like hives. A hive consists of panels of honeycomb. Worker bees secrete beeswax from glands in their abdomen then house bees shape the wax into honeycomb. Both sides of the flat honeycomb panel are made up of six-sided cells of uniform size. These waxed cells are used to store honey and pollen and to raise young.

Show me the honey!

Honey is actually nectar that bees have regurgitated and dehydrated. Yum!

THAT'S WILD!

#3

Golden Orb-web Spider

"Come into my parlor, said the spider to the fly," goes the invitation from a poem by Edward Lear. Of all the spiders, the golden orb-web has the biggest "parlor" of them all. Some can be as much as 20 feet high and 6 feet wide. Because they are meant to ensnare large flying insects, the webs are super strong. In fact, the silk of golden orb-web spiders is the strongest natural fiber known, stronger even than steel of the same diameter. The semi-permanent webs are rarely dismantled and, with minor repairs, can last for several years.

I love to surf the web!

It is possible to continuously draw as much as 2,300 feet of web silk from a golden orb-web spider.

THAT'S WILD!

SPECIAL REPORT:
Spin Doctors

Do drugs affect a spider's ability to make webs? Dr. Hans Peters, a German zoologist, discovered the answer by accident. In 1948, Peters was studying how garden spiders spin their webs. However, the spiders didn't get to work until 4 A.M., so Peters asked Peter Witt, a pharmacologist, for a stimulant that would speed up the spiders' work to a more convenient hour. The drug had absolutely no effect on when the spiders constructed their webs, but the webs they built were distorted. More drugs were later tested, and the one that caused the most distortions turned out to be caffeine—which is found in coffee, tea, and many soft drinks. •

Leaf-cutter Ant

On the march, a line of leaf-cutter ants carries pieces of leaves back to an underground nest. The leaves are 30 times the ants' weight—the equivalent to a human hoisting an SUV. So why are the ants carting such hefty baggage? You might assume they intend to eat the leaves, but you'd be wrong. They have bigger plans. For the ants are really tiny gardeners, and the leaves will become fertilizer for fungus gardens that will feed the larvae.

Leaf-cutter ants build enormous underground colonies as deep as 20 feet with tunnels connecting more than 1,000 chambers. The mounds can contain up to 40 tons of dirt. After the worker ants bring the leaves back to the colony, the nurser workers take over, chewing the leaves into tiny bits of gooey mulch. Then the mulch is spread out, covered with the ants' excreta (that's "poop" to you), and sown with a special type of fungus. After the fungus crop is ready (usually 24 hours), the crop is harvested and fed to the leaf-cutter ants' larvae.

Leaf me alone, will ya?

#1 Termites

No animal on Earth can beat termites that live in tropical climates when it comes to building tall structures. The Macrotermes termites of Africa build their mounds up to 25 feet high. These giant mounds protect the colony by providing a constant, stable temperature, so the underground nests get neither too hot by day nor too cool at night. Networks of tunnels and chimneys allow air to circulate through the mounds.

Inside, most of the nest is given over to the cultivation of fungus, which the termites eat to help them digest food. Other sections include the nursery where termite eggs hatch and the tiny chamber where the queen and male termites live and mate.

In Australia, compass termites build wedge-shaped mounds that run north to south. Mornings and evenings, when temperatures are cool, the flat sides of a mound face the sun, which warms the nest. At midday, when the heat is most intense, the mound's thin edge points toward the sun, preventing overheating. Cathedral termites build 20-foot-high mounds. Some have been occupied by continuous generations of termites for more than 60 years.

You are so over the hill!

4 BUG PARENTS

All parents make sacrifices for their offspring. While bug parents may not sock away money for their little ones' college fund, they do whatever it takes to ensure that their offspring will survive. For some bugs that might mean just hanging around until the eggs hatch. Other bugs, though, go to more extreme lengths. And our #1 bug parent makes the ultimate sacrifice!

#9

Earwig

After mating, an earwig dad takes off and mom is left to tend to a nest of 30 to 50 eggs. She carefully guards the eggs against predators and licks them to remove fungal spores and keep them free from infection. After the larvae hatch, mom brings food or regurgitates her own meals to nourish her brood. Once the larvae can survive on their own, however, her devotion wanes. Any young earwigs that do not leave the nest fast may become their mother's next meal.

#10

Golden Egg Bug

Instead of laying her eggs on plants and leaving, the Mediterranean golden egg bug attaches them to the backs, undersides, legs, and heads of other golden egg bugs, both male and female. It might seem as if this parent is shirking her responsibilities, but actually she's upping the chances for their survival. If left unattended, the eggs would be devoured by ants. When carried by other bugs, the eggs stand a much better chance of hatching.

Earwigs get their name from the popular—but false—belief that they crawl into a sleeping person's ear and bore into the brain to lay their eggs.

THAT'S WILD!

#8

Stinkbug

Not all stinkbugs watch out for their young, but some species more than make up for the others' lack of parental care. One species, aptly named the parent bug, guards her 30 to 40 eggs for up to 20 days and later, the nymphs for several weeks. Another species in Japan goes one step further. When a predator threatens her eggs, this mom goes on the defensive, jerking her body and fanning her wings as she tries to scare the intruder away.

#7

Nursery-web Spider

All new mothers face the problem of how to transport the kids from one place to another. The nursery-web spider mother has an unusual solution. She carries her large egg sac in her jaws. Such a burden makes walking difficult, to say the least, so the spider totters awkwardly on extended legs. When the spiderlings are ready to hatch, she fixes the sac to a stem and surrounds it with silk, standing guard outside the tent-like structure until her young emerge.

#6

Scorpion

Mother scorpions give their offspring a free ride until they are ready to face the big, bad world on their own. Born alive in thin, transparent wrappers, the scorplings break free and scramble aboard their mother's back. Often, the mother scorpion will even turn her pincers sideways on the ground, forming a makeshift ramp for her young. The soft and defenseless scorplings are carried about until their exoskeleton hardens, and should one slip off, mom will nudge it back into place.

What's YOUR sign?

#5 Wolf Spider

This protective mother constructs an egg sac—which can be as large as she is—and attaches it to the silk-producing structures at the tip of her abdomen. She will strongly defend her eggs and, if the sac is removed, she will search for hours to find it. When the spiderlings are ready to emerge, mom bites open the sac and a brood of up to 100 clambers onto her abdomen. Wolf spiders don't spin webs, but wander through their territory looking for food. Wolf spiderlings may ride on mom's back for a week while she hunts. After that, they're on their own.

Wolf spiders are solitary hunters, but they got their name from the mistaken belief that because they often gather in large numbers, the spiders are pack-hunters, like wolves.

THAT'S WILD!

#4 Giant Water Bug

Unlike the majority of female insects, the mother giant water bug has it easy when it comes to childcare. After using mucus to glue more than 100 fertilized eggs to her partner's back, she takes off, leaving him to mind the kids. For a whole month, dad carries his backpack of eggs with him wherever he goes. To make sure the eggs are properly aerated, he periodically leaves his watery home and suns them. Underwater, he rocks his body and bends his legs to pump water over his unhatched charges. At the end of the month, the eggs will have tripled in size.

- To quickly paralyze large prey such as fish and frogs, the giant water bug injects venom that's even stronger than an equivalent amount of venom from a rattlesnake.
- The giant water bug uses air bubbles stored under its wings to breathe underwater.

THAT'S WILD!

Burying Beetle

Burying beetles may well deserve the insect world's award for best co-parenting. Both male and female take active roles in rearing their brood. The action starts with preparing for the little ones' arrival. These beetles can smell a body within an hour of death, from up to 2 miles away. Once the carcass is located, a mating pair will either bury it on the spot or move it up to 3 feet away before burial. Once underground, the beetles remove the dead animal's fur or feathers and roll it up, smearing the body with the beetles' secretions. This keeps the food from smelling as it rots and attracting competition. Next, mom lays her eggs near the carcass. After the grubs (larvae) hatch, she feeds them regurgitated, predigested flesh from the dead animal. At times, dad will also feed the young beetles, but his principal activity is guarding the nest. Both parents leave when their young can fend for themselves.

Burying beetles may be small, but they like their food sources big! Before they became extinct, passenger pigeons were their primary food source.

THAT'S WILD!

Dung Beetle

Mammals can be so wasteful! They get rid of plenty of good nutrition on a daily basis when they poop. Luckily, that nutrition won't go to waste if there are dung beetles around. Dung beetles not only feed on dung, but also use it as a nursery for their kids! One or both parents, but usually the male, roll a ball out of dung that the beetles have located with their keen sense of smell. Dung is a precious resource in the insect world, and the male may have to fight off others intent on stealing the goods. After winning the prize, the beetle pair finds a soft patch of dirt, buries the ball, and mates. The female then lays her eggs inside the ball. Once hatched, the larvae get all the nutrition they need from the dung.

Why doesn't anyone want to play ball?

- Adult dung beetles don't eat dung, but use their mouthparts to suck out the nutrient-rich juices from the manure. The grubs, however, eat everything, plant fibers and all.
- To ancient Egyptians, the dung beetle, or scarab beetle, was revered and viewed as a symbol of renewal. Just as the dung beetle rolled its ball of dung, so did the god Khepri roll the sun across the sky each day.

THAT'S WILD!

#1 Australian Social Spider

When it comes to childcare, this spider mom really goes the limit! Unlike nonsocial crab spiders, she can only reproduce once, but she does her best to ensure that her young survive. She starts by building a nest of overlapping eucalyptus leaves where she conceals an egg sac containing up to 80 eggs. The spiderlings hatch when the weather starts to get warm. As they get bigger, they add to the nest, while mom spends the summer catching insects much larger than she is. After the spiderlings finish feasting, mom eats the leftovers, storing the nutrients from the food in unfertilized eggs inside her body. In the fall, when it starts to get cold and there are fewer insects to catch, it's time for the stored nutrients to do their job. They enter mom's bloodstream—but instead of nourishing mom, they nourish the hungry spiderlings, who suck the enriched blood from mom's legs. When mom is too weak to move, the spiderlings finish her off, dissolving her insides with venom and digestive juices and slurping her up.

SPECIAL REPORT:
Giving Blood

In the ant world, the adults of some species can't digest their own food—they have to be fed by other workers who regurgitate food that's been predigested. In the case of the Dracula ant of Madagascar, the worker ants take this one gory step further: They suck the blood of the nest's larvae, which they later regurgitate for the hungry ant queen. Though the larvae don't die, they have been observed trying to escape when the worker ants appear. •

5 SUPER BUGS

Look! Up in the sky! It's a bird! It's a plane! No, it's super bug! When you think about it, bugs are remarkable survivors. Whether they've evolved amazing defenses to avoid being eaten, found ways to live in the most extreme environments on Earth, or are so adaptable they can survive almost anything, the ten bugs you're about to meet have each earned the title of super bug.

#10

Golden Wheel Spider

When a parasitic wasp approaches a golden wheel spider on a sand dune in Africa's Namib Desert, the spider has to get away fast or become food for the wasp's larvae. What does it do? It tucks in its long legs, flips on its side, and cartwheels down the dune to safety. These desert spiders can really cover some ground. One species rolls at up to 20 revolutions per second, appearing as a blurred ball on the desert landscape.

#9

Puss Moth Caterpillar

This caterpillar has more than one trick up its sleeve when it comes to avoiding being eaten. If threatened, it puffs up its head, emphasizing its large eyespots and revealing a bright orange-red ring that looks like a huge gaping mouth. Its next line of defense is to wave its two whip-like tails (actually modified legs) around. If all else fails, it blasts the predator with a spray of formic acid.

#8

Fog-basking Beetle

The Namib Desert in Africa is one of the driest spots on Earth. Even so, it gets occasional moisture when fog rolls in off the ocean. And when that happens, the fog-basking beetle is ready and waiting. It climbs to the top of a sand dune and facing the fog-bearing wind, lowers its head and raises its rear end as if it were doing a handstand. As fog meets beetle, the mist condenses, drips down the insect's back—and into its open mouthparts.

#7

Coffin Fly

A fly that can live its entire life underground? It may be weird, but it's true. Also called the scuttle fly for its habit of running rather than flying away, this tiny insect can actually tunnel down through cracks in the ground to reach its food source—human corpses. They are most active on corpses that have already begun to dry out a bit, about a year or so after death. Several generations can live while buried underground, as long as they have food to last.

Fog-basking beetles are found only on the western, ocean side of the sand dunes because the fog zone doesn't extend over the high Namib dunes to the eastern side.

THAT'S WILD!

#6

Yucca Moth Caterpillar

The yucca moth has enlisted a plant—the yucca—to ensure its survival. After mating, a female moth uses her long palps (mouthparts) to collect bits of sticky pollen from a yucca flower and roll them into a ball. She then flies to another yucca plant, deposits her eggs inside the flower's seed capsule, and uses the pollen to fertilize the flower, ensuring that her developing larvae will have plenty of yucca seeds to eat. To survive periods of high temperatures and drought, the larvae can halt their growth for up to 30 years until conditions improve.

The yucca plant is also dependent on the yucca moth, its only pollinator, for survival.

THAT'S WILD!

#5

Alkali Fly

Though California's Mono Lake is nearly as salty as the Dead Sea and chockful of harsh chemicals known as alkalis, it teems with life. Alkali fly adults and larvae thrive in this environment, feasting on the algae that form on the lake's surface. The flies not only keep the algae in check (making life easier for the lake inhabitants), but also provide a rich diet for the birds.

When an adult alkali fly has fully developed inside its underwater pupal case, it cracks open its head and a small sac inflates and pops the top off. The sac then deflates, the head reassembles itself, and the fly emerges from the case and swims to the surface.

THAT'S WILD!

#4

Petroleum Fly

A member of the shore fly family—tiny insects that congregate around ponds, streams, and ocean beaches—the petroleum fly, or oil fly, lives in California in naturally occurring pools of oil called seeps. The larvae survive by eating the bacteria that feed on oil. The flies also eat insects and plant matter that fall into the oil. The only time the flies leave their greasy homes is as larvae, pupating on nearby grass stems. At the moment, scientists don't understand how they manage to do this.

Native Americans once gathered the larvae of shore flies for food.

THAT'S WILD!

32

Alpine Weta

Living high in the mountains of New Zealand's South Island, this flightless insect survives the cold by freezing solid! During summer, it finds shelter under rocks and comes out at night to feed. But as winter nears and temperatures drop, the alpine weta, being cold blooded, can't generate enough heat to keep itself warm. Instead, it has found this other solution. It not only freezes solid, but in the process, stops its heart from beating and its brain from functioning. The alpine weta spends the winter months in this state and when the days grow warmer, it thaws out and comes back to life. How does it perform this amazing feat? Scientists are still investigating.

The alpine weta can survive temperatures down to 14°F (–10°C).

THAT'S WILD!

Wingless Midge

Quite a number of insects can stand extremely cold temperatures. Even Antarctica is home to more than 60 of these hardy survivalists. One of them is a flightless midge (there are no flying insects there because they'd just get blown away by all the winds). At half an inch long, this tiny member of the fly family isn't just Antarctica's largest invertebrate but the largest land animal on the entire continent. Penguins and seals may be larger, but they are considered marine animals. The flightless midge is also the only insect to live in this vast freezing desert year round.

> Well, my real name is Margaret.

SPECIAL REPORT:
Arctic Survivors

Arctic beetles manufacture a sort of antifreeze, allowing some species to survive temperatures that dip as low as −188°F (−122°C). The antifreeze is glycerol, a type of alcohol that lowers the freezing point of the insect's blood and prevents ice crystals from forming. As colder weather comes to the Arctic, the beetle reduces the amount of water in its body and increases the antifreeze it produces. Some species have larvae that are up to 25 percent glycerol! •

#1 Cockroach

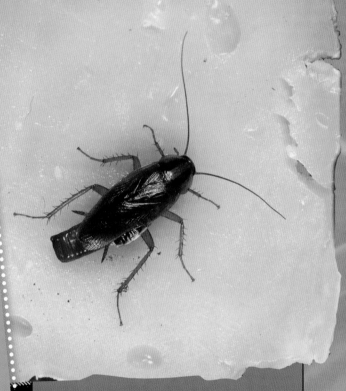

Cockroaches are just about indestructible—ask any city apartment dweller! Supremely adaptable, cockroaches can be found in practically every habitat on Earth, from deserts to grasslands to swamps to rain forests.

These hardy creatures can and will eat almost anything they come across, even wood. Inside their guts are colonies of protozoans, which break down the hard-to-digest cellulose found in wood into nutrients that the cockroaches can absorb. Cockroaches aren't born with these microorganisms—instead, young roaches acquire them by ingesting fecal matter from adults.

Try and catch a cockroach. Chances are it won't be easy. Sensitive to vibrations, a cockroach will scoot for cover long before your hand reaches it. And if you do catch it—even kill it—it won't much matter. Cockroaches are phenomenal breeders. Especially the German cockroach. A single female German cockroach can have over 3,000 babies in its lifetime (less than five months). No wonder roaches have existed for more than 300 million years!

- If a cockroach's head is cut off, it can survive for a week (some say a month) before dying of thirst. One reason is lasts so long is because only part of its brain is in its head, while the rest is spread along the bottom of its body. Another is because it breathes through spiracles, small holes in its body, which aren't controlled by the brain.
- The American cockroach can live for more than four years.
- Resistant to nuclear radiation, German cockroaches have survived blasts of 6,400 rads—six times the amount it takes to kill a human.

THAT'S WILD!

For some bugs, the best defense against predators is to blend in with their surroundings. Other insects prefer mimicry to camouflage. Instead of merely blending in, these crafty creatures modify their body's appearance, taking on the shape of a dead leaf or even a feared predator. Some even go to such extreme lengths as modifying their behavior, earning them the title Master of Disguise.

#9

Leaf Insect

Guess what leaf insects resemble? You got it—leaves. These relatives of stick insects are striking mimics of plants. Their flattened, green bodies help make them indistinguishable from the surrounding leaves. Some leaf insects go a step further, with bodies that look like partially eaten leaves. When a leaf insect walks, it sways a little, so that it looks just like a leaf blowing in the breeze.

#10

Coriplatus Stinkbug

Even to a trained observer, this insect found in South American rain forests is almost impossible to find. Its coloring and subtle markings help it blend almost perfectly into the bark of the lichen-covered trees on which it rests. Known as cryptic coloration, this type of camouflage is favored by many insects. It allows them to avoid predators by blending in completely with their surroundings.

#8

Thorn Bug

With a sharp, spiky extension poking out of their back, certain species of treehoppers look like the thorns on plants, fooling predators into leaving them alone. Found in southern North America, Central America, and South America, thorn bugs are sap suckers, sometimes damaging trees. Some species also secrete honeydew, which can also cause damage.

Do treehoppers talk? A researcher at University of Missouri, Columbia, says treehoppers in the Amazon rain forest communicate through vibrations and that their signals could contain complex messages.

THAT'S WILD!

#7

Hawk Moth Caterpillar

In the rain forests of Mexico, Central America, and South America, this caterpillar blends in with its surroundings when seen from the top. But when threatened, it inflates the front of its body and rears up, revealing eye markings that make it look exactly like the small snakes that live in the same areas. One species from Brazil even waves its head from side to side to further convince the invader to skedaddle.

Some young caterpillars, such as the tiger swallowtail, protect themselves from predators by looking like bird droppings. As they get older, they take on other disguises.

THAT'S WILD!

#6

Mydas Fly

Many species in this family of large flies are mimics of wasps. One species looks just like the tarantula hawk wasp, the fierce predator that can take down the huge spiders which give it its name. The mydas fly mimic even takes on the hawk wasp's jerky movements. Unlike the tarantula hawk wasp, however, the mydas fly is missing a stinger. But, ssssh! None of this fly's predators has to know that.

#5
Carnivorous Inchworm

Like any good actor knows, body language is everything. Hawaii's carnivorous inchworms, which are actually moth caterpillars, have taken this to heart when they go about mimicking a twig, leaf, or bit of moss. A twig mimic grasps the stem of a plant with its hind legs, stiffly stretches its body into the air at an angle, and remains motionless—that is, until a fly or other insect brushes against the sensitive hairs on its back. Then the inchworm snaps around, grabs the bug in its three pairs of front claws, and presto! Instant lunch.

The inchworm has legs only in the front and back of its body. To move, it stretches out its front end, then scoots its back end up to meet it, causing the body to loop like a tape measure. Thus, its scientific family name, Geomitridae, which means "earth measurers."

Anyone got a ruler?

THAT'S WILD!

#4
Aphid Lion

The predatory larvae of lacewings eat a number of soft-bodied insects. However, they are so fond of eating aphids, they are also called aphid lions and purchased by many gardeners to help control these plant pests. Some species of lacewing larvae have a habit of covering themselves under a load of debris and the remains of their prey, earning them the nickname "trash bugs." Little hooks on their back hold the bits and pieces in place, completely hiding the larvae.

Hazel Pot Beetle

#3

The young of the hazel pot beetle have mom to thank for their clever disguise. She fashions pots made out of her own feces and lays an egg in each one. When an egg hatches, the larva remains inside the safety of the pot. As it grows, it adds extra layers of its own feces. It gets around by dragging the pot behind it, its head and legs sticking out from the front. When it wants to hide, it pops its head back into its shell of poop and blends seamlessly into its surroundings. To a predator, the hazel pot beetle resembles nothing more than a small animal's droppings.

#2

Spittlebug

The nymphs of froghoppers, spittlebugs are the spit champions of the insect world. They not only produce "spit" in great quantities, they cover themselves in it. After drinking vast amounts of plant sap, the nymphs blow whatever hasn't been digested out their rears, producing a frothy substance known as "cuckoo spit" that the spittlebugs move around with their back legs. The froth serves two purposes. It hides the nymphs from predators and insulates the bugs, keeping them warm and moist.

A froghopper has been recorded as jumping more than 28 inches into the air. A flea can do the same, but the froghopper is 60 times heavier, making it the true jumping champion.

THAT'S WILD!

These masters of disguise use camouflage and mimicry to fool both predators and prey. Most mantids match the color of the plant they live on, some going so far as to take on that plant's appearance. A mantid might resemble a blade of grass, lichen, a twig, a flower, or a dead leaf. One mantid species that resides in African and Asian deserts looks so much like a stone that it is nearly invisible—unless it suddenly moves. The larvae of another species mimic ants, staying together in large groups so as to increase their chances of survival.

Shall we dance?

- Certain mantids in Africa and Australia are able to switch colors in less than a week. When bush fires sweep across the landscape, these mantids adapt by changing their color from green to charcoal.
- Some mantids look so much like flowers that other insects will land on them to get their nectar.
- The strike of a mantid is so fast that a human can't see it happening because the brain can't process it.

THAT'S WILD!

7 ON THE HUNT

It's a bug-eat-bug world out there. And thank goodness for that! Bugs provide a vital service by keeping down the population of insect pests. The ten bugs on the next few pages are among the most extreme predators of their kind, either consuming vast numbers of fellow bugs or taking down prey the same size or larger than themselves.

#9

Ant Lion Larva

Mostly found in warm climates, this underground warrior digs a funnel-shaped pit in sandy soil and buries itself at the bottom. When unsuspecting prey—usually an ant—falls into its trap, the ant lion reaches up and grabs it. If the prey manages to keep from falling all the way into the pit, the ant lion tosses grains of sand at its victim until it loses its grip and falls.

#10

Ladybug

Aphids are major garden pests, sucking the sap from the leaves and buds of plants and causing major damage. Luckily for gardeners, aphids are the ladybug's favorite food. A ladybug larva eats its weight in aphids each day and an adult can consume more than 5,000 aphids in its lifetime. The ladybug also eats other garden pests, including whiteflies, mealy bugs, and scale insects.

When threatened, a ladybug will roll over and play dead. It also secretes a foul-tasting yellowish liquid from its leg joints to deter birds from eating it.

THAT'S WILD!

#8
Spitting Spider

Unlike most spiders, the spitting spider actively hunts its prey. This tiny spider creeps up on its victim until it's within spitting distance, then ejects, or "spits," two streams of sticky silk in a zigzag pattern over the prey, gluing it to the ground. Venom in the silk paralyzes the victim until the spider gets close enough to give it the death bite. Then the spitting spider removes the silky bonds and enjoys its meal.

Spitting spiders can trap their prey from up to 2 inches away. That's ten times their body length.

THAT'S **WILD**!

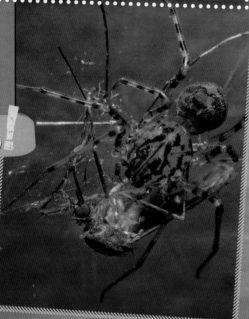

#7
Robber Fly

Swift hunters of the air, these predatory flies chase and catch prey in mid-flight, often taking down large insects, such as wasps, bees, and even dragonflies. Robber flies use their excellent eyesight to locate prey, then zoom in for the kill. After using their piercing mouthparts to stab the victim, robber flies—like many other types of predatory bugs—inject saliva that paralyzes the prey and dissolves its insides, allowing the flies to suck up their liquid meal.

#6
Diving Bell Spider

This ingenious arachnid has found a novel way of adapting to its watery life. Since it needs oxygen to survive, the spider constructs a bubble out of silk, which it attaches to an underwater plant. The spider then makes repeated trips to the surface to collect air on its thick, dense body hairs. Once it has filled the bell with air, the spider waits inside for prey, like small fish and tadpoles, darting out to make a kill and dragging the food back into its lair.

Dragonfly Nymph

Dragonfly nymphs live underwater, careening about by expelling jets of water from their rear. Ferocious hunters, they eat insects, small fish, and tadpoles, catching them in an unusual way. Their scoop-like lower jaw, or labium, shoots out to harpoon prey. The labium comes equipped with hinged hooks that grasp the prey so the nymphs can pull it back to their mouth.

An adult dragonfly zooms above lakes and ponds to search for tasty mosquitoes, consuming up to 100 a day.

THAT'S WILD!

Hello. Are you lunch?

Praying Mantis

With its typical prayer-like posture, the praying mantis looks innocent and humble. But watch out! Appearances can be deceiving. Actually, all mantids, including the praying mantis, are well-designed killing machines. After a mantis uses its keen eyesight to spot its prey, it quickly seizes its victim with its long spike-lined forelegs and holds it in a pincer-like grip. Then the mantis begins its grisly meal—while its prey is still alive! The mantis's lightning-fast speed can bring down a range of prey, from insects to tree frogs, lizards, mice, and even hummingbirds.

- The praying mantis is the only insect that can turn its head from side to side.
- About 800 years ago, a Chinese monk created a type of kung fu based on the praying mantis's hunting stances.

THAT'S WILD!

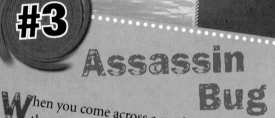

#3

Assassin Bug

When you come across a predator named the assassin bug, you know you are dealing with a relentless killer. Assassin bugs measure between .3 and 1.5 inches long, yet these aggressive hunters often go after prey much larger than themselves. A few tropical species target millipedes as their main prey. At ten times the size of the assassin bug, one millipede poses quite the challenge. That's why several assassin bugs sometimes join forces and attack the giant creature simultaneously.

The wheel bug, a type of assassin bug, gets its name from the cogwheel-shaped structure on its thorax.

THAT'S WILD!

#2

Giant Diving Beetle

The giant diving beetle is well suited to its aquatic lifestyle. Its smooth, streamlined body lets it scoot around the lakes, ponds, and streams it calls home. An excellent swimmer, it uses its hairy hinds legs as oars to change direction. Under its wings, it carries portable air tanks—trapped air bubbles—which it replenishes each time it comes to the water's surface.

Voracious predators, these giant insects will devour any aquatic insects that come their way, as well as frogs, toads, salamanders, and small fish. They use their sharp mandibles (jaws) to tear their prey into pieces.

- At night, diving beetles sometimes take to the air, navigating by the moon's light. They often get confused by artificial light sources and can be found by porch lights and streetlights.
- The offspring of the giant diving beetle are just as predatory as their parents. Called water tigers, the larvae have two large pincers for catching prey.

THAT'S WILD!

In numbers there is strength. That is the strategy behind the success of the army ant. A single ant can be easily disposed of by most creatures. But when faced with a colony made up of hundreds of thousands, even millions of insects, almost no living thing in its path is safe. Army ants are nomadic; they are almost constantly on the move—and on the hunt for food. Found in the tropical forests of South America and Africa (where they're called driver ants), these migratory creatures march at night. Even though army ants have poor vision and are only able to distinguish night from day, they use their superior sensitivity to smells and vibrations to locate and attack prey, stripping insects, frogs, and lizards plus larger prey like snakes, goats, and pigs to the bone. A colony of army ants can eat up to 100,000 animals (mostly bugs) in a single day!

- Soldier ants have such tremendous jaws for defending the colony that other workers have to feed them.
- It's said that Native Americans once used army ants as sutures. They'd hold the ants near the wound and pinch them so their jaws would shut and hold the edges of the wound together. The ant's body was then removed, leaving the jaws in place until the wound healed.

THAT'S WILD!

CHAPTER 8 TRICKY BUGS

"Oh what a tangled web we weave, when first we practice to deceive." This line from a famous poem could have been written for these ten extremely tricky bugs that have devised really sneaky tactics to survive. Our #10 bug uses deception to mate with his beloved, while the trickiest one of them all, a spider, has found many ways to outsmart its prey—fellow spiders!

#9

Snail-eating Caterpillar

In Hawaii lives the only caterpillar that eats snails—and snails only. This moth larva crawls around inside a case it builds of silk with bits of snail shells and debris attached. When it comes across a snail, it traps it by spinning silk strands around the shell. Then the caterpillar wedges its case against the snail's shell, crawls out, and follows the withdrawing snail inside to eat it alive.

#10

Nursery-web Spider

When your intended is much larger than you are, has poor eyesight, and a taste for your own kind, you have to be pretty brave—or foolish—to risk courtship. The male nursery web spider is neither; he's just very clever. Before he attempts to mate, he brings the female spider a special present that he's wrapped in silk—a dead insect. As she eats her gift, the male spider takes his chance and mates.

Cuckoo Wasp

Like the birds they are named after, cuckoo wasps lay their eggs in other animals' nests. These small brightly hued wasps hang around the burrows of their hosts—which include bees, silk moths, and potter wasps—until they get a chance to sneak inside and lay their eggs. This can be dangerous if the host returns and catches them in the act. Luckily, cuckoo wasps come equipped with a hard, pitted outer shell that shields them against stings and bites.

#8

Crab Spider

Crab spiders do not set traps for prey. Instead, they wait for their prey to arrive—sometimes waiting in one spot for days or even weeks. Color is the crab spider's secret weapon. Experts at camouflage, these spiders sit on plants that match their coloration. Some species are even able to adjust their color to the exact shade of the flower.

When gently prodded from its spot, a crab spider scuttles sideways like its namesake, the crab.

THAT'S WILD!

#6

Bolas Spider

Bolas spiders are specialized hunters. Each species goes after only certain species of moths. Moths are good at escaping from webs—their scales stick to the webbing so they can easily break free—so bolas spiders have evolved a sneakier way of catching their prey. They release the same sex pheromone as a female moth of the prey species, tricking the males into thinking they have found a mate. Once a moth is within range, the bolas spider throws out a line of silk with a sticky glob at the end. The moth becomes entangled on the line and the spider reels him in and devours its meal.

Purseweb Spider

Pity the poor bug that lands on this spider's purse—it's in for a nasty surprise! After digging a burrow, the purseweb spider lines it with a long, tube-shaped web. Part of the tube is below ground, but the top part is above ground, hidden by soil and bits of leaves. When prey steps on the trap, the spider bites through the tube and grabs its victim, dragging it inside to be eaten.

- Purseweb spiders spend most of their lives inside their webbed tubes.
- Instead of digging a burrow, one kind of purseweb spider stands its long silken tube against a tree or a rock.

THAT'S WILD!

Ogre-faced Spider

With its two large eyes and long stick-like body, this night hunter is one scary-looking spider. Part of the family known as net-casting spiders, this crafty arachnid builds a scaffold web to use as home base. Then it produces a stretchy band of netting from silk. When the silk net is ready, the spider hangs head-down from the scaffold web with the net held between its four front legs. As soon as prey comes near, the spider stretches the net wide and lunges downward, entangling the prey in the net. The prey is then secured with extra silk and eaten.

Each morning, the ogre-faced spider rolls its old net into a ball and eats it. At night, it weaves a new one. **THAT'S WILD!**

New Zealand Glowworm

Found in caves and crevices throughout New Zealand, this peculiar creature is actually the larva of the fungus gnat, whose transparent skin is bioluminescent, shining with a bluish-green light. After the larva hatches, it uses mucus and silk to create a hammock from which it dangles silk threads that are covered with sticky globs of mucous. The larva emits a soft glow that attracts flying insects that soon become entangled in the sticky silk. The glowworm senses the struggling prey's vibrations and pulls in the line. The prey is then either sucked dry or eaten whole.

- The hungrier a glowworm is, the brighter its glow.
- Should a glowworm enter another larva's tube, the two will fight, sometimes glowing brighter to establish dominance. The loser often ends up as the winner's meal.
- As adults, fungus gnats retain their ability to glow. Females use the glow to attract mates and often lose it after laying their eggs.

THAT'S WILD!

We're always ready for the holidays.

Not all fireflies glow as adults, but all larvae produce light. The larvae, known as glowworms, use their light to alert predators that they taste bad.

THAT'S WILD!

#2

Firefly

In summer, fireflies light up the night in tropical and temperate regions. These glowing insects aren't really flies but beetles, and the reason they pop their lights on and off is to attract a mate. In most species, it's usually the males who fly about flashing specific patterns. The females perch on low-lying bushes, and when they're ready for action, they flash a signal pattern in response. The flash patterns can be single or multiple flashes or they can be a continuous glow. Amazingly, each species has its own unique flash pattern.

It sounds like a fine system, but the females of a few species have a slightly different agenda when they flash. These so-called "femme fatales" mimic the response flashes of other species of female fireflies. The males, duped into approaching the false beetles, are then promptly pounced on and devoured.

SPECIAL REPORT:
Let It Shine!

Inside a firefly's abdomen are organs containing light-producing chemicals. When these chemicals are combined, a reaction takes place that produces light. Unlike most light sources, the bioluminescent light produced in this manner doesn't waste energy and it doesn't produce heat. If you touched a bioluminescent light source, it wouldn't burn your fingers like a light bulb that's been on for a while. •

Portia Jumping Spider

The Portia is one smart spider with a variety of tricks up its sleeve. This group of jumping spiders, which lives in Africa, Asia, and Australia, preys upon other spiders, especially other jumping and web-building spiders. With a body that looks like leaf litter and a slow, jerky gait, the Portia fools jumping spiders into allowing it to move in close enough to pounce. Portias are also known to lure other jumping spiders from their nests with vibrations.

For web-building spiders, the Portia uses a different approach. It produces a special kind of "music" to catch and devour them. By plucking the host spider's web, the Portia makes a variety of frequencies and specialized patterns. It tries out a whole slew of signals. When one catches the host spider's attention, the Portia continues with that signal until the other spider draws near. Then it goes in for the kill, swiftly lunging forward and injecting its prey with venom.

- Portia spiders are very persistent. One spider was observed to pluck at a web for three days. Its patience was rewarded when the host spider finally wandered over and was snatched.
- Most Portia spiders specialize in different hunting methods—either vibration mimicry, nest probing, or covert stalking. But one species, *Portia fimbriata*, employs all three methods.

THAT'S WILD!

9 SPEEDY BUGS

If bugs held their own Olympics, which would take the prize as the fastest runner or the fastest flyer? Luckily, we don't have to wait for such an occurrence. Scientists have done the research for us, and they have come up with some amazing conclusions. Read about these extreme finalists and then give a round of applause to the insect that ranks as our top speedster.

#9

House Centipede

You might expect a creature with 15 pairs of legs to be a clumsy oaf, tripping over its own feet all the time. In fact, the house centipede is a swift and agile predator. Using its wave-like gait, this centipede can scuttle along at 16 inches per second, or about .91 miles per hour. The house centipede has longer legs in the back, and when moving forward, actually lifts these rear legs over the shorter ones.

#10

Mother-of-Pearl Moth Caterpillar

The adage "a rolling stone gathers no moss" is especially true for the larva of the Mother-of-Pearl moth. If threatened or poked, the world's fastest caterpillar rolls itself into a ball and hightails it away. It actually rolls backward, and at a rate of almost 15.75 inches per second, to boot—that's 40 times faster than its usual speed and the equivalent of about .89 miles per hour.

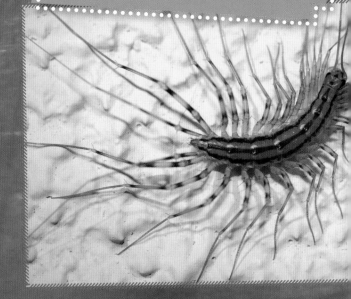

#8

American Cockroach

The speedy American cockroach was clocked at 59 inches per second, or 3.4 miles per hour. That doesn't sound so impressive until you factor in the animal's size. The American cockroach can cover a distance of 50 body lengths in one second! That's ten times better than a human can do in the same amount of time, eight times better than a horse, and three times better than a cheetah, which is considered the fastest animal on land!

#7

Tiger Beetle

Fierce desert hunters, tiger beetles use their incredible speed to chase down prey, such as ants, termites, and other small insects. While all species of tiger beetles are speedy, the fastest is from Australia. The cheetah of the insect world, this long-legged beetle travels at 5.6 miles per hour, or 125 body lengths per second—the equivalent of a 6-foot-tall human zipping along at 511 miles per hour!

#6

Wind Scorpion

As fast as the wind, these scary-looking desert creatures are not actually scorpions but solpugids, another type of arachnid from the group that includes spiders and scorpions. These amazing hunters can travel at speeds of about 10 miles per hour. Once they spot their prey, wind scorpions swoop down on it. With the help of enormous jaws—bigger for their size than in almost any other animal—these creatures can bring down scorpions and even lizards, small rodents, and birds.

The wind scorpion is a speedy eater, too. It can devour a grasshopper in one minute.

THAT'S WILD!

#5

Monarch Butterfly

The monarch is the fastest butterfly, traveling at a record 17 miles per hour. It is also quite the long-distance flier, traveling as many as 2,000 miles. Monarchs spend the spring and summer in the United States and southern Canada. The average lifespan of a monarch born during this period is about two months. Monarchs born in the fall, however, live for about seven months. Soon after emerging from their cocoons, these adult butterflies migrate to the fir forests of Mexico. Gliding on air currents for up to 44 hours before stopping, individuals often rest in the same spots as previous autumn generations. After arriving, the butterflies will produce their offspring and die. Upon hatching, the new generation will mate and then journey north to begin the cycle anew. How do they know where to fly? That's one of the great mysteries of life.

#4

Desert Locust

The desert locust of Africa can fly at up to 21 miles per hour, but could it really migrate across the Atlantic Ocean? For a long time, scientists didn't believe this was possible, because the locusts don't store enough fat for such a long journey. But in 1988, many Caribbean islanders noted the arrival of the African desert locust. The insects were apparently riding a wave of low pressure air that later turned into a hurricane. The length of the trip: nearly 3,000 miles!

Now that scientists know that desert locusts can cross the ocean, they believe that the locust species in North America evolved from an ancestral locust that traveled from Africa.

THAT'S WILD!

Deer Botfly

In 1926, an entomologist reported that the deer botfly flew at the amazing speed of 818 miles per hour. For about 12 years, people accepted his estimation as true. Then, another scientist proved with certainty that this feat was impossible. To maintain such a high speed, the fly would require so much fuel that it would have to eat more than its own weight in food every second! Not to mention that when flying, the fly would produce a very clearly heard sonic boom. Today, scientists have recalculated the tiny insect's speed and have determined that it travels at a quite respectable 25 miles per hour.

Irving Langmuir, the 1932 winner of the Nobel Prize in Chemistry, was the scientist who refuted the deer botfly's flying record. Until he did, this dubious record was reported as true in the *New York Times* and the *Guinness Book of World Records*.

THAT'S WILD!

#2

Dragonfly

This mini dragon of the sky is among the swiftest and most acrobatic of all insects. It can dip, dash, and dart, fly backward as well as forward, and reach a speed of 30 miles per hour. Muscles located at the base of its wings power a dragonfly's flight. In order for its wings to work properly, a certain body temperature must be maintained at all times. Before take-off, the dragonfly warms its flight muscles either by basking in the sun or rapidly fluttering its wings. Overheating is also an issue. When it is too hot, a dragonfly will point its tail to the sun in order to lessen the amount of heat absorbed.

• The dragonfly's wings are marvels of aerodynamic design. Ridged instead of flat, the wings hold air and thereby help generate thrust, or forward movement. Each wing is also capable of moving independently of the other.

• Dragonfly nymphs can remain in the larval stage for as long as a few years, depending on weather and other conditions. Adults usually live for a few months—long enough to mate and lay eggs.

THAT'S WILD!

And for my next trick, a triple flip!

#1 Sphinx Moth

This family of moths is also known as hawk moths and for good reason. Although they are not meat-eaters like the birds, these moths are super-swift flyers, clocking in at speeds of more than 30 miles per hour. Their narrow wings and streamlined bodies allow the moths to zoom through the air. Like dragonflies, the moths warm up their muscles for flight through shivering. Certain species have the ability to hover in midair while feeding, much like hummingbirds. The rapid wingbeats that allow the moths to perform this feat use up a lot of energy, so the moths drink only from flowers producing very sugary, high-calorie nectar.

SPECIAL REPORT:
More Insect Olympians

Runners and fliers aren't the sole athletes of the insect world—there are plenty of high jumpers, swimmers, and weight-lifters, too. A spittlebug, or froghopper, holds the record for longest insect jump at 28 inches. Whirligig beetles zip around the water at high speeds, never colliding with each other thanks to their unique "radar" that detects the wakes of other insects. The rhinoceros beetle is not only the strongest insect, but also the world's strongest animal for its size, able to carry 850 times its weight on its back. To match this, a human would have to tote around 75 cars! •

CHAPTER 10 BUG PESTS

If the FBI included bugs as well as criminals on its most-wanted list, the following insects would have their mugs plastered on posters in the post office. These extremely pesky bugs have rap sheets filled with crimes against human property and natural resources. But don't forget—these "pests" aren't deliberately causing millions of dollars worth of damage but only doing what they have to in order to survive.

#10 Stinkbugs

Members of the insect group known as true bugs, stinkbugs emit foul-smelling chemicals that ward off predators. The plant-eating varieties are also a farmer's nightmare, eating many kinds of crops, from soybeans, rice, and wheat to fruits and nuts. Leaves are filled with holes, stems decay from being covered with digestive juices, and fruit becomes dimpled with "catfacing" caused by an enzyme that stops plant tissue from growing.

#9 Japanese Beetle

Native to Japan and other areas of East Asia, these shiny beetles were accidentally introduced in the United States in 1916. The female beetle lays her eggs in the soil and when the larvae hatch, they feed on the tender roots of grasses and other plants. Adult beetles travel and feed in swarms, chowing down on the flowers, fruit, and leaves of fruit and nut trees, shrubs, and nursery plants.

A swarm of Japanese beetles can strip a fruit tree bare in 15 minutes.

THAT'S WILD!

#8 Dermestid Beetles

The nearly identical larvae of two closely related species, the warehouse beetle and the khapra beetle, are destructive pests of grains and seeds. These bugs are hard to get rid of because the larvae can hide in tiny cracks and crevices and live for several years with little or no food. But when food is around, can these bugs make pigs of themselves! Open a box of infested rice and the grains can seem alive with crawling larvae. Shed larval skins are irritants and can also affect people with asthma or allergies.

I love to go bolling.

#7 Boll Weevil

In 1892, the boll weevil, a native of Mexico and Central America, made its first appearance in Texas. Traveling at a rate of 60 miles per year and devouring cotton all the way, it took the weevil 30 years to make it to the Carolinas. Females do most of the damage when they lay their eggs on the plant's buds and in small bolls of cotton. The larvae hatch and begin to consume the cotton plant, causing the damaged parts to drop. Even feeding punctures made by the weevils can stop plant growth.

#6 Aphid

There are many species of aphids and all are harmful to plants, sucking their sap and causing them to wilt or curl and turn yellow. These rapid breeders are less than one-eighth of an inch long, but they feed in dense colonies. Healthy plants are often able to fight off an infestation, but aphids sometimes transmit diseases when they feed. The species of aphid that spreads a fungal disease to potatoes helped bring about the Irish potato famine of the 1840s, when close to one million people died of starvation.

Aphids excrete excess sap as honeydew, which ants, bees, and wasps collect as food. Certain species of ants even tend aphid colonies, milking the little beasts for their sugary fluids.

THAT'S WILD!

#5

Gypsy Moth Caterpillar

Since the early 1980s, the gypsy moth caterpillar has chomped its way through more than one million acres of forest each year, leaving in its path trees stripped of all their leaves. These larvae feed continuously on the leaves of hardwood trees like oak and aspen. In severely infested areas, you can see tons of the caterpillars crawling up and down the trees and even crossing roads as they make their way to greener forests.

In 1869, the first gypsy moth was brought to Massachusetts by an amateur French scientist. Twenty years later the first full-blown infestation occurred.

THAT'S WILD!

#4

Yellow Crazy Ant

Since yellow crazy ants were accidentally introduced to Christmas Island from Africa or Asia, colonies of the ants have banded together, forming huge supercolonies that prey on the island's wildlife. The ants spray formic acid on creatures much larger than themselves, such as reptiles and crabs, to kill them. To make matters worse, the ants protect scale insects, allowing them to flourish. Scale insects suck sap from trees and excrete it as sweet honeydew, which yellow crazy ants harvest and eat. The more the scale population grows, the more trees are damaged.

- The yellow crazy ant's rapid, erratic movements when disturbed during foraging give it its name.
- Yellow crazy ants have killed as many as 20 million red crabs on Christmas Island.

CRAZY!? You should see his uncle!

THAT'S WILD!

#3 Red Fire Ant

Accidentally introduced in the United States during the 1930s, red fire ants have become a major pest. These tiny stinging terrors have infested more than 300 million acres in the south, the west, and Puerto Rico. Besides damaging farm equipment (they chew through electric wiring), these insects can kill livestock. They also attack people, and they don't stop until they are removed—and red fire ants have extremely potent venom.

One reason red fire ants have flourished is because their natural predators, phorid flies, weren't around—that is, until recently. Florida and Texas have brought in the phorid fly to tackle red fire ants. This fly swoops down on a fire ant and injects an egg in its body, which later becomes food for the developing larva. When the fly larva moves into the fire ant's head, it produces enzymes that dissolve the connective tissue between the head and body, so the head falls off. That's why the phorid fly is commonly called the "ant decapitating fly." When the larva becomes a full-grown fly, it bursts out of the ant's head.

You'll lose your head over me!

It's gotta be around here somewhere.

SPECIAL REPORT: Turning the Tables

In its native Africa, the mopane worm can consume more than 500 tons of plant leaves in less than two months. Despite the fact that this worm— actually the caterpillar of the mopane moth—often eats the leaves meant for grazing livestock, farmers welcome its presence. That's because the large mopane worm is an important protein source for millions of Africans, fueling a huge moneymaking industry. The mopane worms are harvested by hand in the wild. They are then either dried in the sun or smoked to preserve them. The worms are served raw or fried until crunchy. They are even canned and sold in supermarkets. •

#2

Termites

With their voracious appetite for wood and other plant materials, termites are major pests worldwide. Because these insects can digest cellulose, the main component of all plants, they will attack and damage crops, plantations, timber homes, and even furniture, clothing, and books. Found throughout the southern United States, Formosan termites hail from Asia and probably arrived on naval ships returning home after World War II. Formosan termites, sometimes called super termites, devour wood at a rapid rate and live in large colonies in underground nests that spread out as much as 300 feet. In addition to wood, these termites also chow down on paper, insulation, and plaster.

Although termites feast on our crops and possessions, they are necessary to the planet. In tropical grasslands and forests, termites play an important role in recycling. By consuming dead wood, leaves, and grasses, these greedy feeders break down plant material and make it useable once more. It's hard to say thank you to an insect that also chews your favorite baseball bat to pieces, but perhaps we should!

A colony of Formosan termites can consume about 1,000 pounds of wood each year.

THAT'S WILD!

Just call me Queenie.

Desert Locust

A swarm of desert locusts can have up to 50 billion individuals. It's little wonder then that such a huge group can cause extensive damage. Such a swarm is capable of stripping 400 square miles of land of all its vegetation. But the really amazing thing about these locusts is that they won't swarm unless conditions are just right—or wrong, as the case may be.

When rain falls in the desert and food is plentiful, these grasshoppers from Africa and the Middle East live a solitary life. However, in times of plenty, the population increases and when food supplies begin to dwindle, the insects undergo a drastic change. As the creatures crowd together to eat the few remaining plants, their hind legs touch. This contact triggers the change from solitary to gregarious—insects that form swarms. The next time the nymphs shed their skin, they change color from green to yellow and black, and their abdomen shortens. If the drought conditions continue, a swarm is born when these nymphs become adults, and it flies off in search of food, a huge, deadly mass of destruction sometimes traveling for thousands of miles.

- In one day, the weight of food eaten by a swarm of African desert locusts is almost four times that eaten by the entire human population of New York City.
- Up until 1921, people thought that solitary and gregarious desert locusts were two separate species.

THAT'S WILD!

11 ARMED AND DEADLY

The extremely dangerous bugs you'll encounter next don't like to be messed with. If a predator persists in bothering them, these characters have a solution—a painful jab with a stinger full of venom. Many also use their venom to paralyze and kill prey. And if an unfortunate human gets in the way of these creatures' stingers, they'll also suffer from the effect of the venom.

#10

Puss Caterpillar

With its soft gray or brown hair, the puss caterpillar resembles a furry little kitten. But this is one puss you don't want to pet, for underneath all that hair are stiff spines connected to venom glands. Touch this moth larva and the tiny, barbed spines will break off and become embedded in your skin and can cause pain, headache, nausea, and even vomiting.

#9

Centipede

Both indoor and outdoor varieties of centipedes are aggressive predators that go after cockroaches, grasshoppers, and other scurrying insects. Larger species may even take down small rodents! Centipedes have a pair of poisonous claws located directly under the head that they use to capture and kill prey. These claws—once a pair of walking legs that now resemble mouthparts—can inflict a painful bite.

Centipedes and millipedes are not insects or arachnids. They are part of another group of animals called myriapods which means "many legs."

THAT'S WILD!

#7

Tarantula Hawk Wasp

With a stinger that's a third of an inch long, this wasp packs quite a wallop. People who have been stung describe the pain as being almost unbearable. Luckily, the effects last only a few minutes and the venom is not lethal. That's because it's meant to disable specific prey: tarantulas, which the wasps use as hosts for their developing larvae. The neurotoxin in the venom that paralyzes spiders doesn't have long-term effects on mammals.

#8

Red Fire Ants

These South American stinging ants, accidentally brought into the United States, have flourished in the South and Southwest. They build their mounds in sandy soil in pastures, gardens, and fields. If one of these mounds is disturbed, watch out! A swarm of these aggressive creatures will come out to defend the nest, attacking the intruder with multiple stings. Their venom burns like fire (hence their name) and causes tiny blisters to form.

Don't mess with us!

#6

Yellow Jacket

Highly aggressive, the yellow jacket stings repeatedly and with little or no provocation. These yellow-and-black wasps live in colonies and will attack to protect their nest. Certain species build their nests out in the open, while others conceal their nests underground in old rodent burrows. Except for wasps that live in year-round warm climates such as Australia, the colonies die off once cold weather hits.

#5

Bullet Ant

After one sting from this large ant, you feel like you've been shot. Besides intense pain, the venom causes trembling, fever, and nausea. In a few, rare cases, it can even lead to death. These Central and South American ants make their nests among tree roots and are fiercely territorial. If the nest is disturbed, the ants rush out to attack the intruder, making warning noises.

Created by entomologist Justin Schmidt, the Schmidt Pain Index rates insect bites and stings on a scale of 1 to 4. The sting of a bullet ant is rated 4+ and is described "like walking over flaming charcoal with a 3-inch nail in your heel."

THAT'S WILD!

Hello, honey!

Hi, sweetie!

- In 1956, African honeybees were brought to Brazil to improve the honey harvest of the local bees. When the two varieties interbred, the super-aggressive killer bees were the result.
- Even if a victim runs away from an attack, the bees will continue pursuit for more than a mile.

THAT'S WILD!

#4

Africanized Honeybee

Slightly smaller than the average honeybee, an Africanized honeybee is otherwise identical in appearance, but its personality is much different. When its hive is disturbed, this bee becomes enraged and attacks. After the bee stings the intruder, it releases a chemical scent that alerts the other bees to attack. The venom of the so-called "killer bee" is no deadlier than a regular bee's. The danger lies in the hundreds of stings a swarm can inflict. Even someone not allergic to bee venom can die after a massive killer bee attack.

Brazilian Wandering Spider

Instead of being content to stay in a web or lair, the five species of this deadly spider of Central and South America are free-roaming, creeping along the jungle floor at night in search of prey. During the day they hide. In areas where people have encroached upon the spiders' territory, this habit can lead to accidents, for the spiders often scuttle into homes, boxes, shoes, and cars—anywhere where it is dark. If disturbed, these big, aggressive spiders are not afraid to attack. Their bites are extremely venomous and fast acting, but studies indicate that the animals may not use up all their venom with each bite. When they do, however, the results can be deadly. Unless treated, a person can die within 15 minutes.

In the past, Brazilian wandering spiders were sometimes found hiding in bunches of imported bananas, resulting in their being nicknamed banana spiders.

THAT'S WILD!

SPECIAL REPORT:
Venom or Poison?

Although these two words are often used interchangeably, there is an important difference. Both venom and poison are toxic substances; the difference is in the delivery. Venom is injected through spines, stingers, fangs, or teeth. Centipedes, for example, are venomous. They deliver their toxin through their pincers. Poison is a substance that is eaten or absorbed through the skin. Millipedes are poisonous animals. Eat one and you would get very sick. Some creatures pack a double whammy and are both venomous and poisonous. ●

#2 Yellow Fat-tailed Scorpion

The world's most dangerous scorpion, the yellow fat-tailed scorpion, from northern Africa and the Middle East, kills more humans than any other. Like all scorpions, this desert dweller uses its sting, located in the tip of its tail, mostly for self-defense. If its prey is on the large side, the scorpion will also use its venom to subdue its victim. The venom itself is a neurotoxin—a substance that works on the victim's nervous system, causing sweating, an uneven heartbeat, difficulty breathing, and if left untreated, convulsions and death.

- In North Africa, the yellow fat-tailed scorpion kills more than 100 people a year.
- Scorpions can regulate the amount of venom they produce in relation to the size of their victim. A large amount is delivered only when facing large predators or prey.
- Scorpions usually sting as a last resort. Many prefer to make noises to warn off predators.

THAT'S WILD!

#1 Sydney Funnel-web Spider

Commonly considered the world's most venomous spider, this Australian creature's venom is especially toxic to humans and less so to other mammals. Female spiders rarely leave their burrows, so males are the ones to watch out for. When they are ready to mate, they go wandering at night, and because Sydney funnel-web spiders easily dehydrate in the sun, come dawn they scurry to find a safe haven. They look for anything dark, moist, and cool. That might be a crevice in a rock or it might be in a person's garage or shed. To make matters worse, only males have the kind of toxic venom that is so dangerous to humans. They have such a forceful bite that the fangs can pierce a fingernail! The venom attacks the nervous system, first causing numbness around the mouth. Next come nausea, vomiting, sweating, and salivating. Without immediate treatment, the person will fall into a coma and die. Luckily, antivenin is available for this deadly spider's bite. Since it was introduced, no deaths have been reported.

Without a doubt, people consider bugs among the most extremely pesky creatures in the animal kingdom. How many picnics and outings have been ruined by troublesome ants or biting flies? But some bugs are more than just annoying. They can be downright deadly, transmitting and spreading disease. Our number one biter is a common insect that is infamous for causing almost three million deaths a year.

#10

Trap-jaw Ant

These bugs clamp their jaws shut so fast—up to 110 miles per hour—that researchers had to use the same kind of technology to record the motion as they would use to film a speeding bullet! The force of such a bite is so powerful that if a trap-jaw ant bites an object too hard to be crushed, the force of the impact will toss the ant up into the air. Some ants have been seen deliberately biting the ground to produce the same result. Scientists think this may be a strategy to escape from predators.

#9

Giant Water Bug

Next time you dangle your feet in an inviting stream or pond, remember the giant water bug, or toe biter. This large aquatic insect from western North America has a very painful bite. Most of the time, it jabs its sharp sucking beak into prey, which include insects, tadpoles, and small fish. But occasionally it does bite humans—though after a single jab, it usually swims away in search of tastier fare.

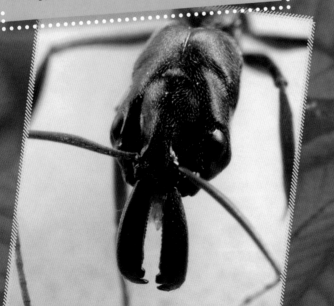

#8

Blackfly

Most people in the United States consider blackflies a summertime nuisance, spoilers of picnics and other outdoor activities. But to people allergic to the fly's saliva, their bites can be deadly. Blackflies also transmit diseases like onchocerciasis, a leading cause of infectious blindness in Africa. Only the females of certain species bite, and due to their bladelike mouthparts, the bites can be extremely painful.

Ahh rare, just how I like it.

#7

Tsetse Fly

These sturdy half-inch-long African flies specialize in feeding on vertebrate blood. It's when they feed on an animal infected with the parasite that causes sleeping sickness that they become a deadly danger. The flies then pass along the parasite to their next victim, which is sometimes a human. Sleeping sickness is a deadly disease, but it is curable if found in its early stages.

#6

Conenose Bug

This mini Dracula from southwestern North America and South America comes out at night to bite its victims. Also called the kissing bug, its bite is painless, so sleepers don't waken as the bug sips from the lips, eyelids, or ears. Some people are allergic to proteins in the kissing bug's saliva and in rare cases go into shock. Many of these midnight Romeos, especially in South America, also carry a one-celled organism, which can cause Chagas' disease, a kind of sleeping sickness.

I love bedtime!

Bedbugs are attracted to warmth and the carbon dioxide in exhaled breath.

THAT'S WILD!

#5

Common Bedbug

"Sleep tight and don't let the bedbugs bite" is a common refrain heard at bedtime. But in way too many households, bite they do. These tiny, wingless nibblers are active at night, crawling out from their hiding places to pierce people's skin and feed for about five minutes at a time. An infestation is extremely hard to get rid of. Think about it: A female can live for as long as year, laying up to five eggs a day. You do the math! The speck-sized nymphs also need blood meals to develop into adults.

#4

Lice

These parasites are wingless and unable to jump, so lice usually spend their entire lives on their host, hanging onto fur, hair, or feathers with their claws. The only time lice change their address is when two hosts are very close to each other or when their host dies. Most lice can only live on one type of animal, and not all lice feed directly on their hosts. Some, called chewing lice, feed on flakes of skin or feathers. Sucking lice, however, use their sharp mouthparts to drill holes and extract blood. Some lice can transmit diseases. The human body louse, for example, spreads typhoid. Other species can pass more dangerous parasites to their hosts.

If lice fall off their hosts, they will die. They need a constant temperature and moisture level—provided by warm-blooded host animals—in order to survive.

THAT'S WILD!

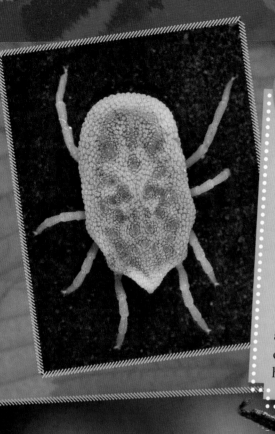

Tick

These parasitic arachnids cause a wide variety of diseases, including Lyme disease and Rocky Mountain spotted fever. There are two basic groups of ticks, hard ticks and soft ticks. Hard ticks have evolved to stay on a moving host. Some hard ticks stay on for as long as it takes to get a blood meal and then drop off, but others stay on one host for their entire lifecycle. Once they latch onto a host's skin, they are almost impossible to remove, especially when feeding. Soft ticks, on the other hand, only go on a host to feed. The rest of the time, they live in the host's nest or burrow.

To find a host, a tick climbs to the top of a plant. When a host approaches (special organs sensitive to humidity and carbon dioxide tell it when), the tick waves its front legs in the air. As the host brushes past the tick, it hitches a ride and attaches itself.

- Hard ticks can take several days to feed off a host; soft ticks can feed in as little as two minutes.
- Hard ticks make a glue in their saliva that keeps them in place while they feed. The glue dissolves when the feeding is complete.

THAT'S WILD!

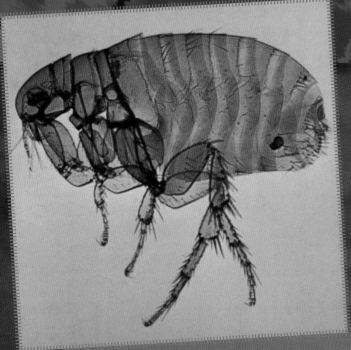

- Human blood doesn't provide fleas with optimal nutrition, so people aren't usually preferred hosts. An exception is the sand flea, or chigger.
- Flea larvae live off digested blood in adult flea feces and other organic matter like bits of skin and hair.

THAT'S WILD!

#2

Flea

These tiny, clinging bloodsuckers are well designed for the job they do. Their streamlined, flattened bodies allow them to scoot easily and quickly around their host. Backward-pointing bristles and sets of spines that form combs anchor fleas in the host's fur or feathers, making them almost impossible to remove. If the host uses its teeth, claws, or beak to fend off the parasite, the fleas' tough bodies prove resistant to crushing. Worse, fleas can also survive for long periods of time without a host. As most pet owners know, it's an uphill battle to get rid of fleas.

Fleas feast mostly on mammals, although a few species are found on birds. When a hungry flea finds an inviting patch of skin, it tilts its head down and its rear up. Then a specialized membrane in its head springs a hammerlike bar that plunges stabbing prongs into the host's skin. The flea continues this plunging action until blood is reached.

SPECIAL REPORT:
A Very Black Death

Fleas spread disease, possibly the worst being bubonic plague. In 14th-century Europe, one in three people died of what became called the Black Death. *Yersinia pestis*, the bacteria that cause bubonic plague, are actually found in rats. As a flea feeds on an infected rat, the bacteria get into the flea's gut and multiply. When the flea feeds on its next host, the disease is transmitted. During the reign of the Black Death, the rats quickly died off and the hungry fleas were forced to find new hosts, including dogs, cats, and humans. •

#1 Mosquito

Far from being mere summertime pests, mosquitoes can be deadly. In fact, these members of the fly family are responsible for killing more people than any other insect in the world. Only female mosquitoes bite, and that's because they need protein from blood meals for their developing eggs. The itching that results is due to an allergic reaction to the mosquito's saliva. Usually, a few uncomfortable days are all that follows. Other times, when the mosquito bites, it may also transmit a small, disease-carrying organism, the most deadly of which causes malaria. Each year, more than 120 million people, the majority living in Africa, fall victim to this tropical disease. One million of those afflicted die. There is no cure for malaria. Mosquitoes also transmit viral encephalitis, yellow fever, and dengue fever.

SPECIAL REPORT:
Fighting Back

It is nearly impossible to get rid of mosquitoes and the disease-causing organisms that live in them because they quickly develop resistance to pesticides. The best humans can do to combat these rapidly breeding insects is to use a variety of control techniques. Applying insect repellent and mosquito netting helps prevent people from getting bitten in the first place. So does keeping the mosquito population down by draining places filled with shallow water where they breed and the larvae develop. ●

Just hangin' around. What're you doing?

Glossary

algae aquatic organisms similar to plants but lacking roots, stems, and leaves

alkali a substance able to neutralize acids

antenna one of a pair of sensory appendages that serve as an organ of touch for insects and crustaceans

antivenin a substance that counteracts the effects of venom

arachnid an arthropod with four pairs of legs and a body divided into two parts; spiders, mites, and scorpions are arachnids

beeswax wax secreted by honeybees and used to construct honeycombs

bioluminescence visible light produced by a chemical reaction inside certain organisms; fireflies and many deep-sea animals produce bioluminescent light

brood animals that hatch at the same time and are cared for by the same mother

camouflage blending in with one's environment due to protective coloring

carcass a dead body

colony a group of the same type organisms that live together

cryptic coloration a type of camouflage that occurs when an animal's color blends in with its background

egg sac a pouch of silk produced by many spiders in which they deposit their eggs

entomologist a scientist who studies insects

exoskeleton the hard outer structure that supports the body of an insect, arachnid, or crustacean

feces animal waste matter or excrement

gregarious social; interacting with others of the same kind

habitat the environment in which an animal is normally found

honeycomb a structure of six-sided cells made out of beeswax that holds the honeybee's honey and larvae

honeydew a sweet liquid secreted by aphids and certain other insects

hemolymph fluid that circulates in insects and certain other invertebrates that functions as blood does in vertebrates

infestation the presence of a large number of pests congregated in one area

labium a lip-like body part that forms the bottom of the mouth of certain insects and other invertebrates

larva the early stage of metamorphosis in many insects when they appear as wingless, often wormlike creatures

mandible a jaw-like appendage near an insect's mouth

microorganism an organism too tiny to see with the naked eye; bacteria and protozoans are microorganisms

mimicry when an organism resembles or acts like another organism or object in order to protect itself from predators

molt to shed an exoskeleton or outer covering such as skin or feathers, which is replaced with new growth

neurotoxin a poison that acts specifically on nerve cells

nomadic moving from place to place in search of food

nymph an early stage of metamorphosis in certain insects in which they resemble smaller, wingless versions of the adults they will become

palp an appendage located near the mouths of insects and certain other invertebrates and which is used to help the animals sense, move, or feed

parasite an animal that feeds and lives off another animal without contributing to the host animal's survival

pheromone a chemical secretion made by certain animals, especially insects, that is often used to attract mates

predator an animal that hunts other animals for food

prey an animal hunted for food by another animal

pronotum the upper plate of the front thorax in insects

protozoan a member of a group of one-celled animals with plant-like characteristics

pupal case a hardened case made by certain insects when they are in the larval stage; the larva changes into its adult form inside the case

thorax the middle body section in insects from which the wings and legs grow

urticating hairs barbed hairs that cover a New World tarantula's abdomen; these hairs can be flicked at the tarantula's enemies; if embedded, they can cause irritation

venom a poisonous substance made by certain animals and delivered through a bite or a sting

wingspan the distance between the tips of an insect's or bird's wings

Resources to Find Out More

Books

Everything Bug: What Kids Really Want to Know About Insects and Spiders, by Cherie Winner, T&N Children's Publishing, 2004

Incredible Insects, by John Townsend, Raintree Publishers, 2005

Insect, by Laurence Mound, DK Publishing, Inc., 2004

Web Sites

Animal Planet
http://animalplanet.com
Official Web site for Discovery Channel's Amimal Planet, featuring fan sites for favorite series, videos, pet guides, games, interactives and much more.

Encyclopedia Smithsonian: Entomology
http://www.si.edu/resource/faq/nmnh/buginfo/start.htm
Links to bugs in the news and other insect resources.

Bug Bios
http://www.insects.org
Photos, articles, and links to the wonderful world of bugs.

Photo Credits

T = Top; B = Bottom; C = Center; L = Left; R = Right

Front cover: © Joe McDonald/Corbis
Back cover, pp. 1, 11L&R, 14L, 20T, 24R, 27, 36R, 40T, 44C, 49T, 59L, 72R: Corel
pp. 3, 4, 20B, 22B, 23T, 67B: Digital Vision
pp. 5, 48R: Daniel Rubinoff and William Haines, University of Hawaii
pp. 6L, 28T, 35B, 58, 67C: Ablestock
p. 6R: Hans Christoph Kappel/npl/Minden Pictures
pp. 7T, 12L, 23B, 41, 53B, 55B: Mark Moffett/Minden Pictures
p. 7C: Nick Garbutt/npl/Minden Pictures
p. 7B: © Patrick Coin
p. 8T: © Jeremy Miller
pp. 8B, 30L, 51: Michael & Patricia Fogden/Minden Pictures
p. 9L: Greg Dimijian/Photo Researchers, Inc.
p. 9R: Pete Oxford/Minden Pictures
pp. 10T, 13C, 37C, 65L: Mitsuhiko Imamori/Minden Pictures
pp. 10B, 24L, 25T, 36L, 48L, 60L, 68T: © Ken Preston-Mafham/www.premaphotos.com
p. 12R: © Reuters/Corbis
pp. 13T, 50B: Piotr Naskrecki/Minden Pictures
pp. 13B, 18L, 43C, 46, 55C, 56B, 59R, 65R, 73T: Stephen Dalton/Minden Pictures
pp. 14R, 66R, 71: Tom McHugh/Photo Researchers, Inc.
p. 15: © François Gilson/BIOS/Peter Arnold Inc.
pp. 16, 43T, 47T, 53T, 56T, 68B: Courtesy Discovery Communications, Inc.
p. 17: Fletcher & Baylis/Photo Researchers, Inc.
p. 18R: Dr. Paul A. Zahl/Photo Researchers, Inc.
p. 19T: © R. K. Walton
pp. 19C, 40B, 49C: © Tom Murray/www.pbase.com/tmurray74
p. 19B: Gerry Ellis/Minden Pictures
p. 21: © Ben Johnston
pp. 22T, 42L, 62T, 63T, 64T&BL, 67T: Scott Bauer/ARS/USDA
p. 25BL: Claus Meyer/Minden Pictures
pp. 25BR, 66L: © Troy Bartlett
p. 26T: Gordan Smith/Division of Public Affairs/U.S. Fish and Wildlife Service
p. 26B: A. Cosmos Blank/Photo Researchers, Inc.
p. 28B: Mitsuaki Iwago/Minden Pictures
p. 29T&B: © Theodore Evans
p. 30R: Ingo Arndt/Foto Natura/Minden Pictures

p. 31T: Paul L. Th. Beuk/www.diptera.info
pp. 31C, 54L: Dr. John Brackenbury/Photo Researchers, Inc.
p. 31B: Dan Suzio/Photo Researchers, Inc.
p. 32T: © Jonathan Armstrong
p. 32C&B: Michael S. Caterino/Santa Barbara Museum of Natural History
p. 33: © Hans Ramløv
p. 34T&B: © Richard E. Lee, Jr.
p. 35T: Nigel Cattlin/Photo Researchers, Inc.
p. 37T: Stephen J. Krasemann/Photo Researchers, Inc.
p. 37B: © Erik Blosser
p. 38T: Darlyne A. Murawski/National Geographic/Getty Images
p. 38B: © Perry Babin
p. 39: © Roger Key
p. 42R: © Leslie B. Durham
p. 43B: Claude Nuridsany & Marie Perennou/Photo Researchers, Inc.
p. 44T: Gary Meszaros/Photo Researchers, Inc.
p. 45T: © Ronald Gaubert
p. 45B: © Paul McNelis/www.BugPhotography.com
p. 47B: Christian Ziegler/Minden Pictures
p. 49B: A.N.T. Photo Library/NHPA
p. 50T: © Marcus Schmitt
p. 52: Gail Shumway/Photographer's Choice/Getty Images
p. 54R: © Callen Harty
p. 55T: © Alan Henderson/Minibeast Wildlife
p. 57: © Philippe Moniotte
p. 60R: © Lynette Schimming
pp. 61T, 64BR: ARS/USDA
p. 61C: Department of Agriculture and Food Western Australia
p. 61B: Bamphitlhi Tiroesele/ARS/USDA
p. 62B: Jan C. Taylor/Bruce Coleman Inc.
p. 63B: Sanford Porter/ARS/USDA
p. 69: © Matjaž Kuntner
p. 70: Tim Flach/Stone/Getty Images
p. 72L: © Alex Wild 2006
p. 73C: © Dr. Jarmo Holopainen
p. 73B: Nature's Images/Photo Researchers, Inc.
pp. 74T&B, 76T&B: CDC/Public Health Image Library
pp. 75T&B, 77T&B: James Gathany/CDC/Public Health Image Library

Index